DWYNWEN
Welsh Patron Saint of Lovers

First published: 2010

© text: Siân Lewis 2010
© illustrations: Graham Howells 2010

ISBN: 978-1-84527-266-1

Cover design: Design Department of the Welsh Books Council

Published with the financial support of the
Welsh Books Council

The publisher wishes to thank Glenda Williams, Anglesey Library Service,
for her kind help.

Published by
Gwasg Carreg Gwalch, 12 Iard yr Orsaf, Llanrwst, Wales LL26 0EH
Tel: 01492 642031 📠 01492 641502
Fax: llyfrau@carreg-gwalch.com
Internet: www.carreg-gwalch.com

Welsh Women
1

Dwynwen

Patron Saint of Welsh Lovers

Siân Lewis

Illustrated by Graham Howells

Long ago, in Brycheiniog in the south-east of Wales, lived a king who had thirty-six children. His name was King Brychan.

Of Brychan's children twenty-five were daughters. Brychan's daughters were among the most beautiful young women in all the land. Noblemen from far and near came to Brycheiniog, hoping to marry them. But King Brychan was a wise man. He would never allow a daughter of his to marry a man who was proud and thoughtless, and many were turned away.

In the north of the country lived a young prince called Maelon Dafodrill. One day Maelon was admiring himself in the mirror.

'I could do with a wife,' he said, stroking his black, silky beard. 'Especially a beautiful wife.' So he gathered a small group of men. They saddled their horses and rode hard for two days and two nights till they reached the kingdom of Brycheiniog.

When they came within sight of Brychan's court at Talgarth, Maelon dismounted by the side of a stream.

'Wait for me,' he said to his men.

He followed the stream a short distance into a wood, where he found a pool that was as still and as clear as a mirror. There he knelt and washed the dust of the journey from his face and hair.

'Ah, that's better!' he said, shaking himself like a dog. 'Now I'm ready to claim the hand of King Brychan's prettiest daughter.'

He smiled at his reflection in the clear water, and with the smile still on his face, he hurried back to his hot, dusty men and rode on.

As soon as Maelon's back was turned, a little boy burst from the bushes, where he had been playing with his sister. The boy's name was Heilin, and he was one of the little princes of Brycheiniog. He rushed up to the pool, splashed water over his face, shook himself, and smiled, just as Maelon had done.

His sister Dwynwen followed him to the water's edge.

'Heilin!' she warned. 'Behave yourself.'

Heilin looked up. His sister was laughing, and combing stray leaves from her hair. Soon Dwynwen wouldn't be playing with him any more, because she was old enough to marry now. 'Did you like that man?' he asked.

'Like him?' said Dwynwen. 'How can I like him? I don't know him.'

'But I heard him say he wants to marry Dad's prettiest daughter,' said Heilin. 'That means he wants to marry you.'

'Me?' said Dwynwen.

'Yes, you,' replied her brother. 'Come on. Let's go home. If I like the man, you may marry him. If not, I'll chase him away with my sword, like our father chased Gwynllyw.' Heilin plucked a wooden sword from his belt, and ran off, waving the sword in the air.

Dwynwen shook her head. Heilin was too young to remember the terrible day when Gwynllyw, king of Gwynllwg, and three hundred of his men had attacked their home and seized their sister Gwladys against her will. In the battle that followed, many men had lost their lives. 'I'm not going to let anyone fight over me,' she said stoutly to

herself, as she set off home. 'I'd rather stay unmarried than let that happen.'

By the time Dwynwen reached the courtyard of the castle, Heilin was playing in the stables. The little boy had soon lost interest in the prince, and was helping to feed the visitors' horses. The men themselves had been welcomed into the hall by her father, the king.

The hall door stood wide open to let in the evening sun. All Dwynwen could see was a jumble of shadowy figures gathered around the table. The men, on the other hand, could see her clearly. What they saw took their breath away. The girl was as beautiful as nature itself. Leaves and blossom danced in her dark, glowing hair. The blush of the sun was on her cheeks, and the twinkle of stars in the blue of her eyes. Maelon's heart began to pound. Never, ever had he expected to fall in love at first sight. But this was it. He loved that girl.

With an effort he dragged his eyes away from her, and turned to King Brychan who was watching him curiously. Maelon knew that the king was a wise and thoughtful man. Some even said he was a saint. In the south-east of the country there were many saints, who went about spreading the word of God.

'I ... I am honoured to meet you,' he stammered. 'I've heard so much about your good work. And your children's too.'

King Brychan smiled. He was proud of his children, many of whom were as saintly as himself. Some had withdrawn from the world to pray. Some had built churches. His son Nudd was even now carrying God's message to

Cornwall. His daughter Cain hoped to set off to Ireland to study with the holy men. Not only was he a father to saints, but a grandfather too.

Yes, he was proud of his children, every single one of them. From the corner of his eye the king watched Dwynwen tiptoe into the hall, and sit quietly in the shadows well away from the table.

Dwynwen had only slipped into the hall to make sure that all was well. She would never forget the king's rage and distress on the day that Gwynllyw and his men had descended on the court of Brycheiniog. That must never happen again.

Her father's calm voice set her mind at rest. The king was deep in conversation with his guest. He was talking about the work of her brother Nudd, and the young man was hanging on to his every word. What a serious and respectful young man he was, thought Dwynwen. Though darker and more rugged in appearance than her father and brothers, his smile was sweetness itself. He smiled at the servants who brought in tapers to light the hall, at the maids who served bread and meat, and at her mother, her brothers and sisters, who joined her father at the table.

She was so busy admiring the young prince, she didn't notice Heilin creep up on her. When he touched her with his wooden sword, she jumped.

'Why are you sitting here in the shadows?' Heilin asked. 'Come over to the table!' Before Dwynwen could protest, he took her hand and pulled her to her feet.

Heilin would have pulled her across to the seat next to Maelon, if she hadn't snatched her hand away and fled to the far end of the table. As she sat down next to her sister Cain, Dwynwen's own heart was beating so fast, she was afraid Cain would hear it. Cain was a calm, quiet person, who had already made up her mind to spend her life in prayer. Dwynwen sometimes thought of following her example. At other times she dreamed of marrying a prince as wise and as kind as her father.

Was Maelon that prince? Dwynwen heard her name mentioned and looked up shyly. Her father was introducing his children one by one to the prince. For a brief moment, before he passed on to Cain, Maelon's smile was for her alone. In that moment Dwynwen fell in love.

While others talked and ate, she watched the glow of candlelight on Maelon's face. Whenever he looked at her, which was often, she did not look away.

At last the meal came to an end. The table was cleared and, as musicians began to play, Maelon got to his feet and walked the length of the hall. He held out his arms, and Dwynwen was swept away, light as a feather and dancing on air. Heilin ran after her, laughing and shouting, 'I told you. I told you,' but all she could hear was Maelon's voice whispering in her ear.

'I love you,' he whispered.

'I love you too,' replied Dwynwen.

'Then we shall be married,' said the young prince. 'Tomorrow I'll ask your father's permission.'

For the rest of the day and night, Dwynwen lived in a dream. From her bedroom window she looked out at the woods and hills of Brycheiniog. Tomorrow she would bid

them goodbye, and ride with Maelon to the north of the country, where snow-capped mountains touched the skies.

The next morning she got up early and dressed in her finest clothes. As soon as she heard Maelon's companions moving around the courtyard, she hurried outside. Some of the men were washing themselves at the well. Some were fastening their belts. Some were leading their horses from the stables. But where was Maelon?

As she approached the hall, she heard the voice of the young prince. He was talking to her father.

'Dwynwen,' said Maelon.

Dwynwen hid behind the door.

'You wish to marry Dwynwen?' her father said.

'I do with all my heart,' replied the prince. 'Do I have your permission to marry her?'

The smile that lit up Dwynwen's face made her twice as beautiful as before. Her father was sure to agree. How could he refuse such a fine young man?

'Tell me this,' said King Brychan. 'Is Dwynwen the fairest of all my daughters?'

'Oh, yes,' said Maelon eagerly.

'So you are attracted by her fair face, and not by the goodness of her heart?'

'No!' Maelon drew back. 'I've no doubt that any daughter of yours is as good as she is beautiful,' he said sharply.

'Then you should always doubt.' King Brychan laid his hand on the young man's shoulder. 'You should never be ruled by your eyes alone,' he said. 'Forgive me, Prince Maelon. I wish you well, but I'm afraid you cannot marry Dwynwen.'

For a moment Dwynwen stood quite still, unable to believe her ears. Then with a sob she turned and fled from the courtyard.

As she ran out of the gate, she heard Maelon cry, 'But why? That's not fair! Your daughter won't find a better man than myself!'

It was true! She would never find a better man than Prince Maelon. She loved him. She loved him with all her heart, and he loved her too! She ran down the path and plunged headlong into the wood where she had first seen the young prince. She and Heilin had made a hiding-place beneath a canopy of bushes near the stream. There no one would find her, and she could cry to her heart's content.

As she pushed her way in amongst the leaves she heard the frantic gallop of a horse. Prince Maelon! He was looking for her. He loved her just as dearly as she loved him. Her father was wrong. She must tell him so. She would take Maelon's hand, go back and beg King Brychan to change his mind.

'Maelon!' she called, as soon as she heard him leap from his saddle.

The voice that answered made her blood run cold.

'Come here,' it bellowed. 'Come here, Dwynwen. You shall be my wife, whether your father likes it or not!'

Dwynwen shrank back into the bushes. Surely that voice wasn't Maelon's. It couldn't be! The creature that burst through the trees had Maelon's size and shape, but his face was a wild man's face, angry and ugly.

Maelon threw back his head. 'Dwyn-wen!' he howled.

'Leave my sister alone.' Heilin came hurtling along the

path, waving his wooden sword. 'Leave my sister alone!' the little boy cried. 'I don't like you any more!'

Maelon brushed the child aside as if he were a fly.

'Dwynwen!' he called. 'Where are you? Ah!' He peered at the bushes. 'I see you!'

With a desperate cry he came running towards her.

Before he could reach her, Dwynwen dropped to her knees. 'Please, God, save us from this madness,' she begged. 'Save us.'

In an instant an angel appeared. He held a cup of golden liquid to her lips, and as she hurriedly drank, her love for Maelon faded away like a summer storm. Maelon's voice fell silent, and a stillness descended on the woods.

For a while Dwynwen too was still. Then she rose to her feet and went to look for the young prince. She parted the branches of her hiding-place, and saw him, standing before her, trapped in a block of ice.

'Oh, poor Maelon!' she whispered to the angel. 'He was rash and hot-headed, but I was rash and foolish too. I don't want him to suffer.'

'Then I shall grant you three wishes,' the angel replied.

'I wish for Maelon to be released from the ice,' said Dwynwen.

At once the block of ice melted away, leaving a dishevelled young man with a dripping beard. Cowed and bewildered, Prince Maelon ran off, called his men and set off for home as fast as his horse could carry him.

'What is your second wish?' the angel asked, as the sound of their hoofbeats died away.

'That lovers' dreams should come true,' said Dwynwen

with a sad, tender smile. 'Or else, their broken hearts should be mended.'

'And your third wish?' the angel asked.

'I wish never to marry,' said Dwynwen.

'Those wishes too will be granted,' said the angel.

Soon after, Dwynwen left the court of Brycheiniog with her father's blessing. She kissed little Heilin, bade her home and her family goodbye, then rode westward to the coast, accompanied by her elder brother Dyfnan and her sister Cain.

At the coast they found a boat waiting for them. They climbed aboard and let the wind blow them wherever it chose. First the east wind blew them out to sea. Then the west wind blew them around Llŷn peninsula towards the isle of Anglesey. On a small island, near the coast of Anglesey, the boat ran aground on a sandy beach.

'This is where I shall live for the rest of my life,' said Dwynwen. 'Here I shall build a small cell, where I will pray to God. If anyone has a broken heart, they may come to me, and I shall do my best to help them.'

On her island, which became known as Llanddwyn Island, Dwynwen built a cell of mud and wood. Her brother Dyfnan left to found a church on the mainland of Anglesey. Her sister Cain went on to found churches in other parts of Britain. Dwynwen was on her own, but was never lonely. She spent her time in prayer and, as the years went by, she was joined by other young women, who had chosen to devote their lives to God.

At the end of her long life, as she lay on her bed, Dwynwen prayed for one last glimpse of the sea. In answer to her prayer a rock that was blocking her view split open,

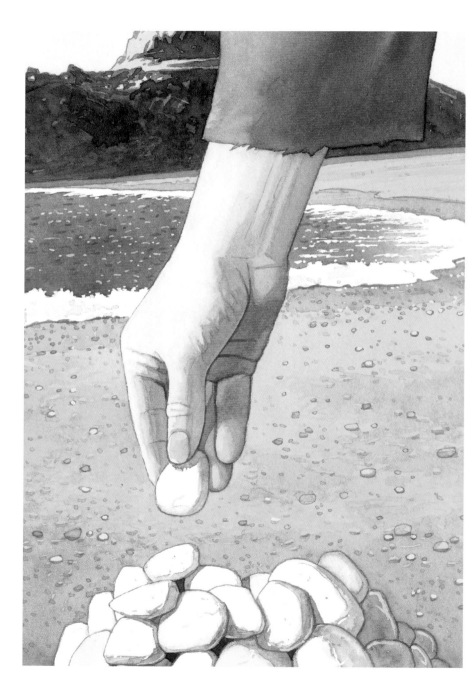

and Dwynwen was able to look out once more at the waves that had brought her to her island home.

Dwynwen died over 1,500 years ago. A cross on the island records that she died on the twenty-fifth of January in the year 465, when she was eighty years old.

The cross itself was built long, long after Dwynwen died, for Dwynwen has never been forgotten. Pilgrims are people who visit holy places, and there are still pilgrims who travel to Llanddwyn Island to pray to Dwynwen, the patron saint of lovers everywhere.

In the old days the sick and the broken-hearted travelled long distances to reach the island in the hope of cure. Some of Dwynwen's belongings were kept in a chest called Cyff Dwynwen. Pilgrims would gather around this chest to pray. Each pilgrim would bring a white stone, and place it on the island.

The pilgrims also lit candles in Dwynwen's honour, and brought gifts of money. A thousand years after Dwynwen's death, this money was used to build a new church on the site of Dwynwen's cell. The ruins of the church can still be seen on Llanddwyn Island, and a service is held there once a year. At low tide the church can be reached from the mainland of Anglesey.

There was a well on the island called Dwynwen's Well. Before praying to Dwynwen, pilgrims would often bathe in it, or drink its water. Some even slept overnight on a rock known as Gwely Esyth, and carved their names in the earth. The water of Dwynwen's Well was said to cure illnesses, such as lung and bone diseases, as well as mend broken hearts.

Many lovesick poets claim to have visited Dwynwen's Well. One hundred and fifty years ago the poet Ceiriog went to the well to try and forget the girl who had broken his heart, but this is what happened to him.

* To Llanddwynwen I went on a fine summer's day
  My poor heart was broken, and full of dismay.
  I drank from the well, and became in a whirl
  Ever more deeply in love with my girl.

  I asked for advice, a man told me to leap
  Straight into the well where the water was deep.
  I sank like a stone, but came up feeling sure
  That I now loved my girl twice as much as before.

Poor Ceiriog! Perhaps he should have tried another well called Crochan Llanddwyn (the Llanddwyn cauldron) which was on a beach close to the island. In this well there were fortune-telling fish. Instead of jumping in, all he'd have had to do was throw crumbs into the water, drop his hanky on top, and hope that the hanky moved. If the fish moved the hanky, it was a sign that the owner would be lucky in love.

At one time, some two hundred years ago, the fish's messages were so complicated that an old lady from the village of Newborough had to sit nearby and explain what

*Adapted from the Welsh

26

was happening. A local girl who came to the well, saw two fish pop out, one from the north side, and one from the south. 'What does that mean?' she asked. 'It means that you will marry a stranger from the south of the county of Caernarfon,' the old lady replied. Some years later, so it's said, her words came true.

Dwynwen's own advice to lovers was much, much simpler. She just wanted people to be cheerful and kind to each other. 'Nothing wins hearts like cheerfulness,' was her message.

Each year on January 25th, St Dwynwen's Day, we remember that message. We send cards to each other that say 'I love you'. What could be kinder or more cheerful than that?

Stories of Welsh Life

An imaginative glimpse of important events in Welsh history told through the experiences of children. Author: Siân Lewis.

1
The Dream
Owain Glyndŵr captures Harlech castle

2
The Prize
A coalmining disaster in Glamorgan

3
Rebecca's Daughter
A girl gets involved in the Rebecca Riots